I0160593

Edith C. Bush

A Memoir

My Faith,

My Family,

My Friends

2022 © Edith C. Bush

All rights reserved

ISBN 978-1-7353828-4-5

No part of this book may be reproduced, stored
in a retrieval system, or transmitted in any form
or by any means, electronic, mechanical,
photocopying, recording or otherwise without
the written permission of the author.

Emerge Publishing Group, LLC

Riviera Beach, Fl

561-601-0349

Cover Photo by C.B. Hanif
Photos by Bentron Personalized Photography
Graphic Design by Mr. Graphic Printing and Design

EDITH C. BUSH 2022

My Faith, My Family, My Friends

Printed in the United States of America

DEDICATION

I lovingly dedicate this book to my parents:

Willie Lee and Gussie S. Coleman

CONTENTS

PREFACE

What is a genius? One whose inspiration demands change. There is no one who has influenced me more. I think about the famous line from Michael Jackson when he was acknowledging James Brown at the BET Awards several years ago. In my family there is no one who has had a greater influence on my, "Life of Service," than my Aunt Edith. She is a tireless worker who has reminded me over and over that we come from a family of fighters and that message sticks with me through many of the small struggles that we face in our daily lives.

Aunt Edith is a graduate of Bethune-Cookman College and now Bethune-Cookman University; but nonetheless, it is a strong HBCU here in the state of Florida with the motto, Enter to Learn Depart to Serve. She has served for more than 50 years and has been a community leader and an authentic individual who I have seen laugh, love and take care of business.

She never really wanted to be directly involved in politics and she tells me that she was getting ready to pull away from a lot of the political issues, but then I had to go and run for office. Me running for office meant that not only would she be involved, but she would be immersed in my campaign because that is what we do for family. The ironic thing about all of this is that after I graduated from FSU with a master's in Urban Planning, she really wanted me to meet Rep. Priscilla Taylor, who she had a very good relationship with because Rep. Taylor was really working on issues related to Black men.

In the '80s and '90s when I was a child, a majority of our family was a lot closer than it is today, one of the negative impacts of social media. I remember a lot of times when many of our family members would meet at Aunt Edith's house for social gatherings, and as children my cousins and I had a chance to become familiar with each other and build a familial bond that is at times lacking from today's generation. Ms. Edith C. Bush is a part of the generation that still holds family in high regard and I can feel that love when I am in her presence, but it is a love that extends to other family members as well.

Things that I have learned from her, you are either here on business or you have no business here at all. She likes to be on time and if you are supposed to give her a ride and are late, she will leave without you. A few years ago when we had a family reunion in Andalusia, Aunt Jenny and Aunt Edith were supposed to be going on a tour together in the morning, but that morning Aunt Jenny was a few minutes late. As Auntie Jenny was walking to the area where she and Aunt Edith were to meet, she saw Ms. Bush leaving on the bus.

It is my saying that a life of service is a life that counts, and I will attest that Aunt Edith has taught me all about service.

Bobby Powell Jr.
FL. State Senator

PART 1

*

My Faith
My Family
My Friends

CHAPTER 1

My name is Edith C. Bush, and I am writing this book entitled "My Faith, My Family, My Friends." I will relate to you as my family. I am very happy that I grew up in a loving family. My parents, Willie Lee and Gussie S. Coleman, were Christian oriented parents. There were six of us children, five girls and one boy. We all were raised as a loving Christian family. My father was a deacon at Mount Maria Missionary Baptist Church. My mother was a missionary in Saint Peter Baptist Church. We all attended Sunday School, we sang in the choir and some of us were ushers.

Into adulthood we continued the spirit of loving the church and praising God.

We had many denominations represented in our family. My mother and father were Baptist, my sister Pauline is a long-time member of the Corinthian Baptist Church in Detroit.

My oldest sister, Willie Lee Coleman was the wife of an AME Minister, who ran for the position and title of Bishop. She was married to Grady Crumpley and they had twelve children.

Ara Jean Coleman Ross was a church going member. Catherine Marshall belongs to St. John Baptist Church in West Palm Beach, and I became a member of the Church of God In Christ, where I was living in West Palm Beach with my aunt. Our spiritual background was very strong.

My brother Alvin Coleman was a Presbyterian Minister. He was also a member of the US Navy, and he was an excellent musician. Pauline Coleman Spears and I were also musicians.

During our early days when our parents were alive, my brother went to Tuskegee University, Paulin went to Paine College, and I went to Bethune

Cookman College. During our vacation at home in Andalusia, AL we were required to play music for the church choir. Summer times, our father was the lawn man for the church yard where he attended and other churches in the area.

My mother was a seamstress: she would prepare the church for their ritual such as the communion service. The family was very church-oriented. Most of us at that time were attending the Mount Maria Missionary Baptist Church in Alabama, the same church where my father was the Deacon.

Usually when we attended church, we stayed all day because the church was a far distance from the house and at night there was little to no lighting to see from the church to our home. We were there for Sunday school, regular worship service, then we would eat lunch after service which was usually between 2pm – 4pm and after the last service we would go home before it got dark.

We were taught the Lord's prayer and the ten commandments, so our behavior reflected that. We didn't cause much trouble in school because our parents were very strict.

EDITH C. BUSH.

CHAPTER 2

My father organized the first family reunion in 1961 and we held the reunion for the Coleman family from Grant River Fall in Andalusia. We held the family reunion annually for over 54 years before the pandemic of 2020 occurred. In spite of the pandemic we still held our reunion which we called a family gathering virtually via zoom. All of our family reunions final activity was church. On Friday night, it didn't matter where we were, which was normally in a different state. Friday night we always did the meet and greet.

The Rule Talk is always done to let the children know that anyone who told them to behave they should do so because we were not going to get put out of any hotel, someone's home, or church during our weekend Friday – Sunday Reunion.

We always enjoyed being together as a family in Andalusia, Alabama, a tiny town 50 miles north of the Florida line, where I was born. The story from the Andalusia Star-News, reports that local blacks had driven to Atlanta to attend the funeral of Rev. Dr. Martin Luther King Jr. Among them, "Will Coleman, cook and chauffer, longtime employee of Mrs. J. G. Sherf Sr."

In addition to cooking and driving for the town white factory owners, he also ran for mayor, lost, and was known until his death in 1986 as the 'black mayor" of Andalusia. Today, the community center bears his name.

"My cousin was a custodian at the white high school," Bush remembers, "and we went to school in a little wooden building and had to wait on a potbelly stove to warm up, but my cousin would go early at the white high school and fire up the furnace so it would be warm."

I remember how we'd be walking to school and here comes the school bus full of white children yelling racist slurs at us as we walked along. And we knew we lived more than two miles from school. Ohh yeah.

By high school, I had gotten my driver's license. I dropped my dad at his boss' gate and watched him walk around the back door. That is when I realized he couldn't go in the front door. Man, that was hard (my throat tightens). But he'd just take it.

In 1950, I graduated from high school as one of the class valedictorians, I went off to Bethune Cookman College in Daytona Beach. I received a bachelor's degree in 1954. My alma mater named me Alumni of the Year in 1999.

After two years of teaching elementary school in DeLeon Springs, FL, I went to Daytona Beach. I arrived in Palm Beach County to travel from school to school in the Glades. Four decades later, I retired as a fourth grade reading teacher at West Palm Beach Northmore Elementray School.

In the meantime I had married, raised a daughter, remarried, earned a master's degree from FAU, and was widowed. I spent my time digging and digging at the roots of segregation and bigotry.

To me, freedom is respect and understanding for other people's culture, and being unified in a spiritual sense – and I don't mean everybody having the same religion. I don't have any problems with people of different nationalities or religions or gay or whatever.

I definitely believe we are making progress, but its important to not take it for granted. I think back on my involvement in Membership of Classroom Teachers Association. Part of that progress is also the Black Educators Caucus who was a delegate to their conventions.

In previous years the CTA convention featured a display offering tips on how to get schools involved in holiday celebrations. They had nothing honoring Dr. King, so when I got home, I started searching and that year with help from Fredeva Nelson, principal of Riviera Beach High School, she put on a program honoring Dr. King. The program was held on Saturday.

I always enjoyed being with my family. It may be my biological family, my church family, or a friend of the family. Family reunions are always exciting. Many of our friends attended because they have few family members, or they do not have family reunions. We hold our reunions in various states and locations. It depends on who is the host.

My parents, Willie Lee and Gussie S. Coleman organized the first Coleman Reunion in the year 1961. We were also encouraged to memorize the 23rd Psalm, the Lord's Prayer, the Ten Commandments and the Negro National Anthem: Lift Every Voice and Sing. These parental sessions instilled good morals and respect for the elders. That inspired good behavior in us all.

Our family enjoyed playing baseball, jump rope, hopscotch, hide and seek, marbles, puzzles, and basketball. Our parents encouraged us to sing in the church or school choir, or usher in the church.

For our family, while living in segregated Andalusia, Alabama, weekdays were workdays. On Friday and Saturday nights, we would go to black-owned restaurant/bar and the adults would enjoy drinking and dancing. Sundays were always for attending church all day. All day church included: Sunday school, morning service, lunch on church grounds, evening service and journeying back home. The church was so far from where we lived, we had many disadvantages. There was little or no light along the road in the community.

I came to West Palm Beach to live with my aunt Ophelia Willard. I attended the Church of God in Christ. The rules were strict—no dancing, cussing, smoking, or drinking. We were taught to believe in the Biblical teachings. The church family was Pentecostal and believed in shouting, speaking in tongues, and the power of the Holy Ghost. However, as a family we attended the same denomination that any family member attended, or where ever we were invited. We were community activists and were associated with Muslims, Jews, Catholics, and other denominations. In fact, in Andalusia the Methodists owned the Brick Church and shared alternate Sunday Services with the Baptist Congregation.

Church officers in our family included: Pauline Spears, Usher Board; Alvin Coleman, Presbyterian Minister; Edith Bush, Mother Board; Willie, First Lady/Pastor's Wife; Will—Father, Deacon; Mom– Gussie, Missionary and Catherine Ara Jean, Church Attendee.

My relationship with people of various cultures improved through my travel to Africa, Cuba, Jamaica, China (Hong Kong), Japan and various US states. In Palm Beach County there are 87 nationalities. I became aware of this by serving on various boards such as:

14

Area Agency on Aging – PBC
Literacy Coalition
Equal Justice Commission
Progressive Northwest Neighborhood Association
Urban League
NAACP

My community activities reflect my father's community involvement as President of the Local NAACP. He attended the funeral of Dr. Martin Luther King Jr. A street in Andalusia is named for my father (Will Coleman Community Center). My father was known as the Black Mayor of Andalusia. Community children often visited our home especially on holidays because my father, who was also a cook would have cookouts and bar-b-ques on our property.

I never stood a chance of not becoming a community leader. As an 90-year-old West Palm Beach resident, I soaked up my family identity and led a storied life that has taken me from the roots in the deep south during the turbulent civil rights movement to a life as a college graduate, teacher and as executive Director of Martin Luther King Jr. Coordinating Committee.

I am a founding member of the committee which started off as the Black Educators Caucus in 1971, but changed as the membership became more diverse, merging with the Women's International League of Peace And Freedom.

Today, I play a key role in the community by leading the committee in its annual month-long Martin Luther King, Jr. celebration that includes art exhibit, performing arts, oratorical, poster, and essay contest, interfaith religious service, gospel fest, tennis or sports tournaments, candlelight services and the scholarship breakfast.

We are able to identify and provide scholarship to students who exemplify artistic, cultural and leadership skills. The students go on to college and empower their communities. The committee also hosts a spring health fair for seniors and a summer peace camp for the youth.

CHAPTER 3

I am deeply passionate about the mini causes the committee has committed to, including the volunteer-driven Martin Luther King, Jr. Coordinating Committee Caregivers Program that provides services including help around the home, food distribution, respite care and transportation—especially to the polls—to those 55 and older.

We live by the scripture— "Feed the hungry, clothe the naked, and if someone is thirsty give them water." For me, the committee brings like-minded people together around Dr. King's message.

Our members belong to various clubs, civic and religious institutions, and we operate as the Martin Luther King Jr. Coordinating Committee family. I believe that a person should be judged by the content of their character and not by the color of their skin. We love and support, empower and promote artistic and cultural programs in my community. I give all the credit for my intrinsic philanthropic nature to my family upbringing from Andalusia, Alabama.

I grew up in a close-knit Christian family during the days of segregation and my home was the do-drop-in. This means people would come in to receive food items including hot meals while enjoying the family atmosphere. My family was always a giving family. There was always something to eat or clothing to provide for anyone in need.

My father worked for the mayor as a cook and chauffeur while my mother was a housekeeper and seamstress. We were the very first family to have electricity in that area and the first to have water from the city. I think it was because my father worked for an influential man who was the mayor of the city.

My parents who had six children, recognized their children were not receiving a good education in the one room school heated by firewood, so I was sent to live with my aunt in West Palm Beach Florida.

I later returned to Alabama, graduated from Covington County training school as a valedictorian and Bethune Cookman University in Daytona Beach where I receive a bachelors in elementary education in 1954. I received my master's in education from Florida Atlantic University in 1975.

I was inspired by my fifth-grade teacher to become a teacher. I taught music at the Glades camp school in Canal point, Pahokee and Belle Glade and was then transferred to the Palm Beach County coastal school and then to Northmore Elementary from where I retired in 1987.

The main reason that I love teaching is it inspires others and promotes creativity.

PART 2

*

Testimonials

My Family, My Friends

CHAPTER 4

Testimonial One

On January 15, 1990, I attended my first Martin Luther King, Jr. Coordinating Committee's Breakfast at the Urban League in West Palm Beach. During the event I noticed that the young ladies who were serving breakfast struggled to maneuver between the rows of tables. After the breakfast I went forward to introduce myself to the chairwoman of the event. During the conversation I mentioned the possible need for a larger venue. She told me that the MLK, Jr. Coordinating Committee simply couldn't afford it. I said you can now and offered to pay for it. A smile came upon her face as she accepted my offer of $1,000 from Fidelity Federal for the following year's breakfast.

The chairwoman was Edith Coleman Bush. Thus began a 32-year friendship which will continue forever. My role in the MLKCC changed rapidly from being the breakfast sponsor to becoming Co-Chair of the MLK Landmark Memorial Park.

The story of the memorial began when Edith challenged WPB City Commissioner Mary Hooks, "Why doesn't West Palm Beach have an MLK memorial?" at the 1995 breakfast. Mary Hooks then led the way to City approval of the project and became Chair of the project. Shortly thereafter Mary was appointed as the Secretary of Labor of the State of Florida and headed to Tallahassee. I then was in charge of the effort to develop and finish the Memorial under the guiding hand of Edith C. Bush.

- Several hurdles had to be cleared before possible construction:
- Selection of architect and builder
- Conceptual drawing (included changes of course)
- Selection of sculpture (image/artist)
- Budget (it was always underestimated)
- Sponsorship opportunities (Lots of arm twisting, guilt and pressure sometimes needed.)
- Construction schedule (often delayed)

The most important question was "Where would we be able to build it?"

West Palm Beach was a part of the Jim Crow South until the late 1960's. The population was pretty much a railroad track society. White folks lived east of the tracks and black folks stayed on the west. After dark you had better know your place.

In order to find a location MLKCC faced the question of private land with unknown costs and zoning issues or city properties that were primarily parks. The size of the memorial dictated the land needed. So the Committee loaded into a mini-bus for a tour. After our thorough review we selected the Currie Park location. The memorial would then be located on Flagler Drive and the Intracoastal Waterway. The site had historic meaning. During segregation, Currie Park was whites-only with the expectation that "negroes" could be there if they worked for white families. After dark, the park was off-limits to the black community.

One of the members on the MLCC, John Clayton, a community leader, told me after the dedication, "This park was closed to us back then and look, it's on the water overlooking Palm Beach!"

I truly believe I was blessed to meet Edith and love her dearly.

David Hochstetler

CHAPTER 5

Testimonial Two

What can we give to the Lord He doesn't already have? He owns the cattle on a thousand hills and the earth itself in all His fullness. What more is left? The greatest thing we can give to God is what he gave to us our entire life, placing ourselves in His service.

I beseech you therefore, brethren, by the mercies of God, that ye present your bodies a living sacrifice, holy, acceptable unto God, which is your reasonable service. Romans 12:1 KJV

Edith and I were the youngest of six children, with Edith being five years younger. You wouldn't know that this force to be reckoned with, in today's Palm Beach County, was a very quiet, tomboyish child. While we older girls were fussing with our hair and dressing up, Edith remained studious and interested in her books.

Our household lacked a television when we were growing up. We gathered our news and listened to different programs from one household radio. It would be no surprise to find Edith listening to sports programs. Her love for sports, especially baseball, continues to this day.

Edith was quiet, but she could also be a little mischievous and daring. I think back to the time when the family had a cow named Betsy. There were certain areas the cow was supposed to be placed in at the end of the day. One day, Mama asked Edith and me to bring in the cow. We asked her where she wanted the cow to be placed. I'm certain Mama didn't have time for foolish questions because her response was, "Just bring her into the house if you want to." With me pulling in the front and Edith pushing at the rear, we pulled the cow into the house!

As children, Edith and I walked to church together. When I look back on this, I realize it was a long way. However, at the time it didn't seem like such a long walk. We had each other for company.

That close relationship was interrupted when Edith was sent, at a young age, to live with our father's sister in West Palm Beach. Our aunt had no children and spent many years helping to raise her nieces and nephews at varied times. Edith lived with our aunt until she went to college. She returned to West Palm Beach after college and has resided there ever since.

If anyone were to ask me to describe my sister, I would say she is "faithful, unique, service-oriented, bossy, firm, exact, and loving." She says what she means and she means what she says.

Edith definitely does not have any feelings of being inferior. You should hear her on the phone when she is talking to legislators and people in authority. I often ask myself, "Why can't she say this in a different way?" But then, she wouldn't be Edith. She commands respect and she receives it. There are often calls of "Ms. Bush. Ms. Bush. Ms. Bush" when she attends public gatherings.

Edith has a special yearning for helping young people as evidenced by her leadership of young people's activities under the auspices of the Martin Luther King, Jr. Coordinating Committee. Also, did I not mention she is "crazy" about Rev. Dr. Martin Luther King, Jr.? She is "crazy" about Martin Luther King, Jr.

Last, but not least, I am glad to be Edith's older sister. I'm proud of what she does; she does it so well.

I hope the Lord will continue to bless her.

With love,

Pauline Spears, Sister

CHAPTER 6

Testimonial Three

E dith C. Bush: It seems like no matter where I am, someone asks, "What is Ms. Bush like?" Am I to answer in a sentence; maybe a few minutes; and hour; even a day? Ha. To answer, it could take a month! Edith C. Bush, my compassionate, loving and kind, activist, best friend, sister-like, a mentor, and a colleague.

She is a black woman, African American, whose ancestors and her God have blessed with body, mind, heart, and soul to raise the village when needed. She has been graced with the beauty of unconditional love and laughter, and, in turn, she touches all persons who have come into her life, especially the children.

As a young child and throughout her teen years in Andalusia, AL. Edith joined her mother and father in community service to individuals and families in need and in being agents of change around neighborhood issues.

At college at HBCU Bethune-Cookman College, Edith Bush stayed active as a member of the college choir.

In over 40 years as an educator, Edith C. Bush, BA, Ed; MA. Ed., found that her passion, fueled by her faith, really was in teaching, inspiring, and motivating all children to both prepare for life and discover their talents through education.

I met Ms. Bush soon after she founded The Matin Luther King, Jr. Coordinating Committee, Inc, (MLKCC), a nonprofit organization, over 40 years ago. She is still serving, at 90 years old, as Executive Director in a non-paid position! True to herself and her God, she is a volunteer for life!

MLKCC was initially a tutorial and after-school program and expanded to sponsor oratory, poster and drama contests commemorating Dr. King's January birth date until the focus enlarged to activities all month in January ending with a Scholarship Breakfast, one of Ms. Bush's greatest legacies. She and all of MLKCC are so proud of the lives now lived by the youngsters involved in the activities and awards of the breakfast. Now MLKCC has activities all year long.

Special to Ms. Bush's heart is the summer peace camp for low-income youth to learn ways to build self-esteem, create peace in their lives and develop a respect for a diverse community, linking them with activities based on the philosophy of Dr. King.

There is a MLK Caregivers program that provides volunteers to assist sick and shut-ins with basic needs. The mission of MLKCC is for multicultural, community outreach and education in all its program centered on philosophy and strategy of Dr. King to address freedom, equality and justice by providing services, pushing for change, or nonviolent protesting. The jewel in the crown of MLKCC is construction of The Dr. Martin Luther King, Jr. Landmark Memorial Park, located on Flagler Drive, one of the largest memorials for Dr. King anywhere in the Southern United States. The park contains plaques, bricks, benches commemorating Dr. King's life and speeches. The highlights are a bronze sculpture of Dr. King backdropped by cascading water on a granite wall and the display of flags, representing great influence in Dr. King's life, waving over the intracoastal towards Palm Beach. I would like to add that at the time of our serious discussion, it was still Jim Crow time here, and the park site was on 'the white-side of the tracks'.

Yes, Edith C. Bush dedicated her personal and professional life, at an early age, in trust to others, so that that one day, our world will become "The Beloved Community," (coined by Rev. Dr. Martin Luther King, Jr.) a community in which everyone is cared for, absent of poverty, hunger, and hate; a realistic, achievable goal that can be attained; and love, trust, and nonviolence will triumph over fear and hatred.)

My dearest friend, Edith, captured the imagination of me and thousands of others through her lifetime of activism to this goal. Everyone who knows her talks first about her passion in every single thing she does; then the twinkle in her eye; the crazy, contagious laughs and giggles; and, of course, the loving kindness one can actually feel coming from her heart! Along with family, friends, and the community, I love Edith C. Bush!

Susan Owen Glaser

CHAPTER 7

Testimonial Four

I have known Edith for over 50 years. We were both teachers in the Palm Beach County School District. We were also both active with the Teachers' Union at the local, state and national levels. This participation also included being engaged in the Black Educators Caucus. Not only did we improve our skills, but we assisted other teachers to be aware of the various resources available to Educators.

Edith naturally embraced this concept because it aligned with her upbringing. Edith often speaks of the lessons she learned growing up in Alabama. These lessons, learned from her family, her Church, and her community, have allowed Edith to structure a program honoring trailblazers in the Civil Rights Movement.

In 1971, the Dr. Martin Luther King, Jr. Coordinating Committee was organized initially as the Black Educators Caucus, sponsoring a remedial tutorial program in cooperation with the Minority Mental Health Association. In 1975, the program became an afterschool program at Friendship Baptist Church in West Palm Beach. The program then expanded with help from the West Palm Beach Housing Authority, Children's Services Council, Community Foundation, Front Porch, and the Pleasant City Neighborhood Association. Edith was collaborating before it became the buzz. Edith recognized that many hands make the work easier.

Edith is an accomplished musician, and she has shared her talent and commitment to cultural activities with her students. This vision laid the groundwork for the Martin Luther King Jr., Coordinating Committee. As Executive Director and Founder, Edith Coleman Bush moved forward with a dream to have an array of cultural events honoring the legacy of Dr. Martin Luther King, Jr. After the early start in the 1970s under the Black Educators Caucus umbrella it was time to look to an independent organization. The MLKCC filed formally in 1988 as an organization.

Still moving forward, Edith was already looking to expand. Now her focus was to include Senior Services. In 1995, the Martin Luther King Caregivers was established as a project to provide services to elderly persons. It is volunteer-driven (like all the MLKCC projects) and gives over 35 trained homemaker assistance; food distribution, respite care and transportation to a target population of 100 economically disadvantaged homebound elders, 55 plus years of age living in the inner city of West Palm Beach.

I don't know how long I've been involved with Edith. As people who know her understand, she has a role for you to perform and it often is very fluid. She has the vision; you must move as you are choreographed. Edith is my friend. I know of her commitment to the actions required concerning an MLKCC Theme. 2022 – The Theme was "Injustice Anywhere is a Threat to Justice Everywhere." Edith Coleman Bush has lived a life with actions that reflect belief in these words.

Edith's behavior reminds me of the song – We've come this way by Faith, leaning on the Lord. Trusting in His Holy Word. He never failed me yet…

Cinthia Becton

MORE TESTIMONIALS…..

"I want to wish you a Happy Mother's Day!

May God continue to bless and keep you safe and with a sound mind. People like you make it so easy to love. I am so grateful for the times we shared, the many times you have been there for me. Thank you for over 20 years of support and love. You are very much appreciated! In addition, I value the lessons you taught me. They are invaluable to me and will be forever cherished, just like you!

I love you to the moon and back!!!!"

Sabrina Cornish - MLKCC Member

***

"Mrs. Bush and her committee are truly dedicated to our community and the legacy of Martin Luther King. She is a leader and an icon who is treasured by so many."

Jeri Muoio - Great Cities for All

***

"The absolute best in commemorating the legacy of Dr. Martin Luther King Jr. providing recognition to outstanding students in the community and supporting issues that affect the under-served populations in our communities."

Denise Albritton - Bus One LLC, Charter Bus Company

***

"Great Service!"

Jay R - JR Capital Groups

***

"In my opinion, Edith Bush is working with one of the finest organizations in our county, honoring the most outstanding peaceful civil rights leader we have ever seen."

Steve Oldham - Unseen Rewards LLC

***

"They are absolutely phenomenal and an awesome asset to our communities and thus the world! Grateful for what they do!"

Letitia Ruffin - The Afri-Touch, LLC

***

"This committee, honoring the great MLK, is carrying on the legacy and Keeping the Dream Alive..."

Serlina James - Creative Solutions

***

"Edith is a tireless advocate for her community and civil rights in general. highly respected..."

Mikki Royce - TMG Writes

***

"This organization has been at the forefront of the Annual MLK Celebration for 40 years"

Robert Dillingham - Robert Dillingham Nonprofit Consulting

PART 3

*

Views In the News

CHAPTER 8

Jewish Community Honors Dr. MLK, Jr. C.C.
By Lou Musmeci; Jewish Journal

As Edith C. Bush was searching for different organizations to share an event honoring the fallen civil rights icon on his birthday, she found comfort in familiar community— the Jewish community of Palm Beach County.

Bush, who serves as Director of the Martin Luther King Jr. Coordinating Committee, had a challenging task this year planning the freedom celebration held on January 16 at the West Palm Beach Temple Beth El. This event was a joint effort between the Martin Luther King Jr. Coordinating Committee, and the Jewish Community Relations Council of the Jewish Federation of Palm Beach, and Temple Beth El.

"This is our first year working with Temple Beth El but we have worked with many other temples and the JCC in the past," Bush said. "Our theme is continuing the civil rights movement for all."

Congressman Alcee L. Hastings (D- Florida) delivered greetings at the ceremony. Hastings said that events such as the freedom celebration are vital to "keep open dialogue."

"There has never been two races that ever received the brunt of intolerance like black and the Jewish community," Hastings said.

For Mark Talisman, President of the Judicial Foundation, an organization which creates exhibitions of Jewish themes, attending the freedom celebration at Temple Beth El was not a first. He attended Kings march on Washington DC in 1963. "We didn't' expect more than 500 people and 385,000 showed up," Talisman said of the 1963 march. "It was one of the most glorious moments on earth."

Talisman was appointed by President Bill Clinton as founding vice chairman of the US Holocaust Memorial Council and Museum to plan, develop and open a 300,000 square-foot museum memorial on the mall facing the Washington monument. He currently serves honored academic and conscious committees.

Prior to the celebration at Temple Beth El, many participants met at Curry Park in West Palm Beach, in front of the Dr. Martin Luther King, Jr. Landmark Memorial, which stood just below in American flag. The American flag was centerpiece of many flags that were all waving due to a cool breeze provided from the adjacent water. Bush led all attendees and sporadic onlookers in a spirited rendition of the Negro National Anthem "Lift Every Voice and Sing." The group closed by singing "We Shall Overcome" and then moved on to Temple Bethel.

Bush was happy to see the different ethnic groups represented at the park and was especially pleased to see everyone singing. "An event like this has to be multicultural," Bush said. "Dr. King said that all of us need to walk together HAND–IN–HAND. These celebrations certainly bring us closer."

Mayor of South Bay, Clarence Anthony, echoed those remarks and said that he attended many events such as the freedom celebration and maintains they are vital to assisting in community relations. "It clearly brings everyone together –" Anthony said. "It also provides an opportunity for everyone to get to know each other as individuals."

The impact by the black community on Palm Beach County was represented at the freedom celebration through the Hudnell Exhibit, which was coordinated by Ineria Hudnell. This exhibit highlights contributions black citizens have made toward the development and history of Palm Beach County. It was on display at the temple's main hall and was visited by attendees prior to the celebration. While looking at the exhibition some attendees were seen gazing at pieces of memorabilia and were brought back in time to a memorable place in history.

"We are just trying to remind our children of where this community came from," Bush said of the exhibit.

CHAPTER 9

Bus Trip Takes Supporters to President Barack Obama Inauguration

By Julyssa Albuquerque and Jonathan Simmons

South Florida Times

Washington DC – Three-year-old Elise Wilson knew President Barack Obama would win reelection and she wanted to see him when he did. So her mother, Antoinette Wilson, made a promise. "She was saying, I want to see Obama." Said Wilson, 34, who lives in West Palm Beach with Elise and her brother Eric, 7, and I said, "OK, if Obama wins, we will go see Obama." So that's the only reason I'm here.

Wilson joined up with 37 other members and supporters of the Martin Luther King, Jr. Coordinating Committee at the Church of God in Christ in West Palm Beach early Sunday morning, January 20, 2013, for the 24-hour bus ride that would take them to Washington DC for Obama's second inauguration.

The trip was organized by Mrs. Edith C. Bush, Executive Director of the nonprofit organization that she cofounded in 1971 to petition for better conditions in segregated schools.

Bush, former educator, and longtime activist took a group to the last inauguration and was planning this year's trip before the election results were announced.

Obama's election was especially important for young people to see, she said, because it showed them what an African-American can achieve.

"There are those of us who know what the dream is about,"she said. "We feel we need to teach our children, especially those born during integration, what it is all about."

Terrell Evans, a high school senior who started volunteering for the committee in middle school, got off the bus with the other travelers at the Robert F. Kennedy Memorial Stadium in DC at 7:30 AM the next day. Evans, who was 18 at the time, said he had never been to an event this important.

But in September the previous year he stood in line for three hours to see Obama speak at the Palm Beach County Convention Center. Evans had anticipated the DC trip for months. "I've got something to tell my kids," he said. "I feel like I am a part of history."

The walk from the stadium to the national mall took nearly 3 hours. Police barricades blocked off streets and herded the hordes around the mall, only to dead end at the Washington monument, more than a mile from the inaugural platform on the Capitol steps. Stadium size sound systems were to bring the grand year to the 800,000+ strong, but transmitted only distorted images and garbled audio. "We walked all this way and we can't see him," said Evans. Elise Wilson was happy, "Where is Obama? Where is Obama?" She asked as she waited with her mother at the monument. Her mother picked her up so she could see above the crowd and pointed at the image of Obama on the TV screen.

"Can you see him now?" she asked. Elise looked up at the big screen and smiled and said "Yes."

"Edith took a really big challenge," Ellington said. "She has done a fantastic job and I admire her courage. Local festivities have grown immensely over the years that Bush has been involved. She has always targeted them toward children and youth."

"They are really too young to know what the civil rights movement was all about," she said. "They are enjoying the fruits of that movement, and this gives us an opportunity to expose them to the real meaning of it."

"If young people really knew what people went through, they would be much more inclined to better themselves." Bush's cozy home in the quiet West Palm Beach neighborhood of Clear Lake is a testament to her and her families' achievements.

Plaques and trophies adorn in the walls and sit on top of the piano in her living room. Family portraits filled the bookshelves. A copy of the cookbook her father wrote lies on a table, and a photograph of the sign naming in Andalusia Alabama Community Center after him rest nearby.

"I think I got my activism from my father," Bush said Will Coleman was a chauffeur and cook by vocation and the unofficial "black mayor of Andalusian" by avocation. "Our house was the hub of the black community" she said. Bush's father was president of the local National Association for the Advancement of Colored People chapter and later a member of Andalusians Housing Authority. If politicians – black or white—wanted to be elected in Andalusia, she said, they came to her father for support.

She is a member of the board of the West Palm Beach branch of the NAACP, the Palm Beach County Literacy Coalition and West Palm Beach Code Review Committee. She also is active in her church as well as the Martin Luther King, Jr. Coordinating Committee West Palm Beach.

Bush's hometown is just 85 miles from Montgomery, where King began his preaching. She attended Bethune Cookman College in Daytona Beach in the 1950s. The school— both its faculty and student body—were integrated, she said.

Off-campus, however, discrimination was everywhere. "When I left school, I had difficulty dealing with it," Bush said. She participated in civil rights marches in Daytona Beach and West Palm Beach. "And I am still a protester." She said, "Our groups will have to keep in front of the young people. That won't be discouraged. The fire of coals is still there."

For 32 years, Bush taught music and reading in Palm Beach County schools. She retired in 1987. Her husband Alvin died in 1985. She has a daughter, son-in-law and two grandchildren who live in West Palm Beach.

Throughout her life, Bush has remained dedicated to children. Each child who participates in any of the King activities will be rewarded for his or her efforts. She sees to that. "It gives children a chance to express themselves artistically," she said.

When this year's event (1991) concludes, Bush will immediately start on next years. She will never give up the fight or the dream.

CHAPTER 10

Leadership Palm Beach County

By Leadership Links

Of all the vacations you've taken what has been your favorite destination and why?

My favorite was a visit to a synagogue in Africa during the summer of 2000. The trip was sponsored by the Palm Beach County School Board multicultural organization. We took educational supplies to the schools there. It was the most exciting time of my life, and teachers and children were so thankful. They appreciated having pencils of their own. They have been sharing pencils.

Can you imagine that? During the trip we toured the island of Goree and experienced the history of slave trade.

Edith C Bush, Executive Director Martin Luther King Jr. Coordinating Committee.

Saint Marks Episcopal

The Martin Luther King Jr. Coordinating Committee recently launched its scholarship and competition events for the 2007 2008 school year. Students in third, fourth, and fifth grade competed in the "Accentuate the Positive, Eliminate the Negative; Fulfill the Dream" essay competition. Winners were: third grade, Lauren Tkaczow, First place: Jordan Barry, second-place: Morgan

Brown, Third-place honorable mentions Kate Mantee, Nicholas Reno, and Christie Vogelsang.

The students and their families were invited to attend the annual award breakfast, which was held on January 21, 2008 at the West Palm Beach convention center.

CHAPTER 11

All I remember is Martin Luther King Jr

By Sanjay Bhatt

In West Palm Beach, whites and blacks came together Saturday to remember the Reverend Dr. Martin Luther King Jr.'s dream.

More than 35 people gathered near Currie Park at the memorial to the slain civil rights leader to hear fiery oratory and sing songs of freedom.

The chanting of "We Shall Overcome" recalled the shock and sadness following King's fatal shooting on April 4, 1968, as he stood on a balcony at the Lorraine Hotel in Memphis.

Organizers hope to draw attention not to his death, but his dream. They pointed at a rising trend of hate crimes and apathy towards civil rights as evidence of the need for more education.

" We are so caught up in the here and now that we've forgotten the there and then," said Kashif Powell, 18 years old at the time. "We don't even care about the struggles we had to go through; just a step in that store to buy those shoes."

The event, "Remembering the Dreamer", was organized for the third year by the Martin Luther King Junior Coordinating Committee. The committee sponsors art, writing, oratory and music every January and awards scholarship to the top prize winners, according to Edith C. Bush, the Committee's Executive Director.

Bush said the committee is raising money to keep the flags flying over the memorial. The flags must be replaced every six months.

47

CHAPTER 12

Rights Struggle Echoed King's Work

By Lou Salome - P. B. Post

Social and political fragmentation, along with the corruption wrapped by money, have destroyed the unity and power that Martin Luther King, Jr. and his allies generated in a segregated society, said Edith C. Bush, Executive Director of the Martin Luther King, Jr. Coordinating Committee in West Palm Beach, and former teacher.

"Nowadays, we're not united for one cause," Mrs. Bush said. "Everyone's in his own little world. It's almost like people are afraid to mention peace, justice, freedom, because the definitions have changed so much. People say they are doing things in the name of freedom; you do what you want as long as it satisfies you. Freedom and segregated society meant equality. Now it is more selfish. It's what I want.

Mrs. Bush believes that black leaders in corporate America have undermined black Americans. Easier access to money has corrupted leaders, black and white, she said, and successful blacks often forget their origins. Her criticism is sharp, pointed: "African Americans are going to have to unite themselves.'

"We've made tremendous progress. But there is still a widening gap in wealth," Mrs. Bush said. "Every child needs a computer at home. That technology is the gap between the wealthy and those who are not."

The Martin Luther King, Jr. Coordinating Committee/Black Educators Caucus was organized 1971 and its members included retired teachers, community leaders and teachers in affiliation with the Palm Beach County Classroom Teachers Association and the National Education Association. Organizers have implemented mini-school and community objectives, including:

1972 – a remedial tutorial summer program (sponsored by Minority Mental Health Association). 1975-1978 - a community remedial program - Reading, science, Health education, mathematics) Friendship Baptist Church.

1979 – present sponsored minority project (Poster contest, oratorical and dramatic presentations) commemorating Martin Luther King week, brotherhood month, summer tutorial program, artistic performances, Afro arts participation, and Palm Beach Community College multicultural festival.

The community has benefited from the various projects initiated by the organization with its emphasis on improving human relations. Community civics, religious, fraternity, sorority and other groups have joined in the support and sponsorship of its annual King Week celebrations.

Sponsorships from banks and other financial institutions provide scholarship for art, oratorical, essay, and music contest. Participating students have gone on to major colleges and universities and have demonstrated outstanding skills, talents, and academics. Many continue to perform in local, regional, and national competitions.

A year-round project includes the sponsorship of students to a weeklong summer camp in which students learn about various cultures and how to respect the diverse contributions of all cultures to a community. The camp exposes the students to theater, arts, crafts, sports, workshops, and music to show ways in which they can live in harmony with all people in nature. MLKCC expands on the teachings and philosophy of Dr. Martin Luther King Jr.

The organization encourages libraries to exhibit the contributions of African-American art year-round and encourage cities to observe the third

Monday of each year for the celebration of King's Birthday as they would any other national holiday. The City of West Palm Beach and the MLKCC recently sponsored Randall Robinson Executive Director of TransAfrica, as the King Week speaker. Other speakers have included multi-millionaire attorney Willie Gary, rabbis, priest and other notables. The Palm Beach Post, Miami Herald, and Sun Sentinel, some of Florida's major newspapers, have provided coverage, scholarships, and personnel for the event.

The schedule of events for the King Week celebration include a kick off reception held at the Classroom Teachers Association, student art exhibit at a major county library complex, performing arts, oratorical, arts and essay contests, an interfaith service, tennis tournament, candlelight service, gospel fest and an award breakfast, and voter registration is an ongoing part of year-round activities of Martin Luther King, Jr. Coordinating Committee.

CHAPTER 13

Joyful Noise Sunday in West Palm Beach Celebrates King

By Elliot Kleinberg – P. B. Post

January 19, 2015

People were moved to stand when Elder Moses Porter said, "This is not just for a show y'all. This is a service." And they responded to his "God is good" by shouting back, " Yes, he is." Nods came when he said, "We're going to celebrate. We're gonna sing. We're gonna dance. And we're going to shout." Barbara Horne, from the Martin Luther King Jr. Coordinating Committee of West Palm Beach, said "We want you to sing like you've never sung before thinking of Dr. King."

And by the time Brent McFadden was singing, *Every Praise is to Our God*, he had the 100 or so people at Orthodox Zion Primitive Baptist Church, all standing.

Sunday afternoon "Gospel Fest" was one of 10 events planned for this weekend by the committee. For decades it has organized events linked to the civil rights leaders birthday said Executive Director Edith C. Bush before the program.

The theme for this year's activities is "We are on flight 2015." This groups motto: Pursue a positive dream. Believe it. Achieve it.

On Monday, the committee holds its 34th annual scholarship and awards breakfast at 7:30 AM at the Palm Beach County Convention Center. It also held "A Unity Interfaith Service" Friday night in Jupiter and a performing arts event Saturday at Roosevelt Middle School in West Palm Beach.

"The civil rights movement began in church" Bush said, noting that the early movement by King and other leaders started from their pulpits at various houses of worship. But she said while Sunday's event focused on the black Christian gospel singing tradition, one of the things that made the civil rights movement work is that everyone joined in.

And she noted that Palm Beach County is home to scores of nationalities and more than 100 languages, all of which need respect. Dr. King said, "Judge a person by the content of their character," Bush said. "We really believe that."

CHAPTER 14

Annual Breakfast Honors King's Legacy

By Jennifer Sorenture - P. B. Post
January 20, 2015

Nearly 800 community leaders and local politicians gathered Monday at the Palm Beach County Convention Center to honor the legacy of Martin Luther King Jr. They were given a yearlong challenge to help local children and young adults find and pursue "a positive dream."

West Palm Beach City Commissioner Keith James, one of the first speakers at Monday's Martin Luther King, Jr. Coordinating Committee Scholarship Breakfast, urged those in attendance to follow in King's footsteps and work with the "next generation to unlock their imagination."

James asked everyone in the crowd older than the age of 30 to work with 12 young people during the next year. "That is only one child per month," James told the packed room that included local dignitaries such as the West Palm Beach Mayor Jerry Morial, Riviera Beach Mayor Bishop Thomas Masters and Palm Beach County Mayor Shelly Vanna.

"We have to take back our children's imagination," James said. "Our kids can achieve more. They can be more than just being a rap star or an athlete."

The breakfast was the 34th annual event, which started even before King's Birthday became a national holiday. The breakfast honors the work of King, along with other people who have made a difference in the community. It also rewards students for skills such as public speaking.

Author Elvin Dowling, the keynote speaker at the annual breakfast, pointed to the racial unrest that swept across the country after the fatal shooting of unarmed teen Michael Brown in Ferguson Michigan, and the fatal chokehold use on Eric Garner in Staten Island, New York.

"A new American revolution is taking place," Dowling told the crowd. "Today the revolution will not only be televised, it will be computerized."

Edith C. Bush, Executive Director of the Martin Luther King, Jr. Coordinating Committee, which organizes the annual breakfast, also pointed to Ferguson. Bush said this year it was important for those in the crowd to reflect on the recent racial unrest across the nation.

Several local chiefs of police attend the breakfast, a move Bush said was meaningful, especially for the children and young adults in the crowd. "We need to encourage these children to be leaders in the community," Bush said.

As part of the mission, Martin Luther King Jr. Coordinating Committee's annual birthday celebration of King includes essay, art, performing arts, and photography competitions open to all students, Bush said

Shannaleen Camy, a first grader at RJ Henley Christian Community School in Riviera Beach and one of this year's winners of the committees oratorical contest, said she practiced her speech for about a week before delivering it to Monday's crowd. The six-year-old needed a step ladder to reach the podium, but that didn't stop her from sharing her dream of becoming a doctor with those in attendance.

"I will pursue it, believe it and achieve it", Camy said in her address.

Camy's sister, Sherwin, a sixth grader at RJ Henley, took first place in the committees essay contest for middle school students. "The contests are important ways for young children to learn about King's life. Sometimes people don't know about the past," Sherween said.

CHAPTER 15

John Lewis's Legacy Lives on in County Activist

The death of John Lewis, the 80-year-old congressman and civil rights icon, was mourned across the country Saturday. For many the greatest tribute to his legacy has been this year's wave of Black Lives Matter protests, which Lewis saw as a continuation of his civil rights battles. Lewis told CBS news last month he was touched to see hundreds of thousands of people, outraged by the police killing of George Floyd, "take to the streets to speak up, to speak out, to get into what I called good trouble."

Longtime civil rights leader Edith C. Bush of West Palm Beach said she sees the reflection of Lewis's early activism in the Black Lives Matter movement. Just as Lewis's legacy emerged from the 1960s protest, she predicted new leaders will emerge from this summer's protest.

"We have to support the young people involved in this new movement," she said. "We've got to nurture strong leaders who will continue his legacy, what he fought for, and what he died for." At 89, Bush says the congressman's early activism resonates with particular clarity in her memory. Seven years older than Lewis, she was born two hours south of Selma, in Andalusia Alabama. But she didn't meet Lewis then—she met him decades later in West Palm Beach at a campaign event for US Representative Alcee Hastings. Lewis had come to lend support to his congressional colleague, Bush said. "I will never forget meeting him, oh" she said. "I still have his picture in my house."

CHAPTER 16

MLK Speaker's Olympic Gold Medal Proves Nothing that Cannot Be Achieved

By Joe Capoizzol – P. B. Post

At 77, Lucinda Williams Adams still enjoys running. And when she jogs through the Cypress Lakes retirement community in suburban West Palm Beach, a few of her neighbors have any idea they're watching a woman who won a gold medal at the 1960 Olympics. "Unless someone asked me, I don't talk about it. I don't want to sound like I'm bragging," she said.

Adams made an exception Saturday night, sharing her story to about 100 people at a candlelight service at greater Antioch Missionary Baptist Church to honor Dr. Martin Luther King Jr.

"There is nothing that cannot be achieved if you are willing to work hard for it," she said before opening a leather case and holding it up to the crowd.

"Who would've thought I would be the proud owner of this gold medal?" The crowd, a mix of all ages, erupted in cheers.

"When I think about her, I think about Jesse Owens and Jackie Robinson, all of the ones who broke the barriers," Edith C. Bush, Executive Director of the Martin Luther King, Jr. Coordinating Committee, said before the service.

Bush said Adams was chosen to give the keynote speech "to inspire our youth to become leaders and to adhere to what Dr. King said, that you judge the person by the content of their character not by the color of their skin."

Adams witnessed the civil rights struggle as she grew up in Bloomingdale, Georgia just outside Savannah, eating in the "colored" sections of restaurants and avoiding parts of town where she might run into trouble.

After graduating from high school in 1955, she competed all over the world with the Tiger Belles, The Tennessee State University women's track and field team. She competed in the 1956 Olympics in Melbourne, Australia.

In 1958 she won two gold medals at the first US versus USSR track and field meet in Moscow on a team that also competed in Hungary, Poland, Greece, Germany, and England.

It was at the 1960s Olympics in Rome when she won a gold medal as a member of the 400m relay team with three other Tiger Belles—Wilma Rudolph, Barbara Jones Slater and Martha Hudson. Adams ran the third leg and passed the baton to Rudolph, who also won two individual gold medals. "It's not about the medal," Adams told the church crowd. "It's about what's in here (pointing to her head) But most of all what's in here (pointing to her heart)."

In an interview before her speech, Adams— who recently retired after more than 30 years as an educator in Dayton Ohio—said she never met King. She still regrets the decision she made as a teenager to not participate in demonstrations with other African Americans.

Adam says she was warned by Tennessee State University Officials that she and other Tiger Belle teammates could forfeit their athletic benefits if they were arrested.

"I am still haunted by that," she said. "Here I am 16, 17 years old. People around me said you and your team can make a difference by competing."

CHAPTER 17

2009 Women of Excellence Awards

By Delta Sigma Theta Sorority, Inc.
The Social Action Award

Edith C. Bush learned the commitment to serve her community as a little girl raised by her parents who were community leaders. Her service started as an elementary school student in Andalusia, Alabama volunteering at the Will Coleman Community Center, named for and dedicated after her father.

A retired educator, Edith C. Bush has never abandoned her commitment to serve the community. Over 28 years ago, Mrs. Bush organized and founded the Martin Luther King, Jr. Coordinating Committee in an effort to hold fast to the perpetuation of Dr. King's ideals of equality among all race and promote the belief of democracy. Of the mini projects of the MLK, Jr. Coordinating Committee, Mrs. Bush has spearheaded the annual King Celebration for over 20 years leading to the establishment of the Martin Luther King, Jr. Landmark Memorial Park on Flagler Drive in West Palm Beach Florida.

Since 1995, she has served with the MLK Caregivers, providing direct service to elders in the community. The MLK Caregivers Project provides over 35 trained volunteers for caregiving, homemaker assistance, food distribution, respite care and transportation to over 100 economically disadvantaged homebound elders. In 1997, Martin Luther King Caregivers was expanded to serve as a food distribution center.

It is amazing with this 71-year-old Jewel in our community can do. She volunteers up to 10 hours a day many days and has done so for over 25 years. She has committed to literacy and is a reliable board member for The Literacy Coalition working with reading programs and activities for local youth, primarily African-American. She is a Board of Directors of the NAACP, Secretary Treasurer Of The National Business League, and Secretary of the Classroom Teachers Association.

" I consider it my duty to my community to help those not as fortunate as I. It is my hope that my volunteerism will affect the country as a whole and individual lives."

CHAPTER 18

President Barack Obama Inauguration 2013

Modern Day Freedom Riders Head for the Capital

By Barbara Duarte – P. B. Post – January 20, 2013

Catherine Fulton decided to bring her grandson on a bus trip to see Monday's inauguration of President Barack Obama so he could feel what she felt in 2009.

"The feeling inside you, even before the president came out, was indescribable. Everybody was crying, and we were holding hands with strangers, with people we didn't know. Fulton at the time was a 61-year-old West Palm Beach resident. She teared up as she recalled the moment Obama took the oath of office.

"He was the first African-American male to become president, and I never thought I would see that in my lifetime," she said, "I want to take my grandson to witness so he can have this experience and share with his own children."

Fulton and her 11-year-old grandson, Maximus Fulton Durrant of West Palm Beach, joined 36 others willing to spend about 24 hours on a charter bus to Washington DC no more than 12 hours in the national nation's capital and another 24 hours on the return bus trip, also to see Obama begin his second term.

The trip was organized by the Martin Luther King, Jr. Coordinating Committee of West Palm Beach, which sponsored a similar journey in 2009 when Obama started his first term.

The 44 passengers consider themselves the heirs of the freedom riders movement of the civil rights era.

In 1961 the freedom riders began when a group of blacks and whites boarded a greyhound bus in Washington and rode to the segregated south.

"In the south, they were so programmed against desegregation they didn't want to see that," Edith Bush, who organized the trip and was among the Coordinating Committee's founders, said Thursday. They said, "You're not supposed to be integrating a group of kids in a bus, so we're gonna burn you down."

More than five decades later, the committee's bus carries the mostly African-American group with a handful of Latinos and white, to see a president who looks like most of them.

"Now we are going from West Palm Beach to Washington on an integrated bus," said Bush, who was on the bus Sunday. "So we are the freedom riders. We are free to ride everywhere on the bus."

Eunice Louis Ferdinand heard about the bus trip the day before it was to leave. There were no spots left, but she gave her phone number to Bush. A couple of hours later, Bush called to say she had a spot.

"I'm happy I can come at my age. I'll probably never see this again," St. Louis Ferdinand. At the time, was 66, a West Palm Beach resident who volunteered for the Obama campaigns in 2008 and 2012.

Fulton anticipates a smaller audience for today's festivities, but she thinks the Presidents message will be greater.

"I want to know what he expects from us," Fulton said. "No president gave us guidelines before. He does it and I feel part of it."

1999 Palm Beach County Giraffe Award Presented

The Women's Chamber of Commerce of Palm Beach County has presented the giraffe award to three local women who have stuck their necks out to serve the community.

They are: Nancy Graham, the former West Palm Beach mayor who is leadership help put the community in the national spotlight; second awardee Nancy Talbert Smith, a Pahokee school teacher who founded women's forum, a mentoring program for girls; and third award is Edith C. Bush, who is a community volunteer and local activist for more than 55 years.

These awards were presented during the fourth annual women's history month celebration in Palm Beach Gardens.

CHAPTER 19

"This time is different,"

Says Activist Who Lived Through Jim Crow

By Carol Rose P. B. Post – July 4, 2020

Edith C. Bush was born in America when gas station bathrooms were marked "white men," "white women," "colored men," "colored women." And that's if Black people had restrooms at all.

Nowadays, the 87-year-old looks on with joyous wonder at the marches that have taken place after the killing of George Floyd on May 25 and Minneapolis while he was in the custody of police officers, one of whom knelt on Floyd's neck for almost nine minutes.

She ponders those marches as well as her years in the segregated south. She could not try on a dress in a clothing store until she was in her 30s- yet, the struggles, the great race divide, continues.

"Young people need to realize," she says, "this wasn't a long time ago."

From Alabama to West Palm Beach

Bush, the youngest of Willie Lee and Gussie S. Colemans six children, was born on July 11, 1932 in Andalusia Alabama, about 75 miles south of Montgomery.

Her father was a chauffeur for the town's mayor, a cook and President of the local NAACP, and her mother was a housewife and seamstress.

Bush, a West Palm Beach resident who has been executive Director of the Martin Luther King Jr. Coordinating Committee since it began in 1981, has established credentials as an activist in the pursuit of King's ideals.

She led the push for The Martin Luther King Landmark Memorial Park, which now sits along the intercoastal waterway in Currie Park, just north of downtown West Palm Beach.

Bush told the Palm Beach Post in April 2000, shortly before the first phase of the monument was unveiled, that she still remembers the ugly faces, taunting and spitting on her in 1954 when she was a 21-year-old Bethune Cookman college student marching in Daytona Beach. She remembers how hard it was to get an education.

She welcomes the involvement of "more open-minded people" of all races in the protest and cites this as a key reason why "this time is different."

Harkening back to Martin Luther King Jr. Bush says, "The dream was for a moment, but our success is the movement toward eradicating systemic racism."

CHAPTER 20

Black leader still disagree: Is answer Integration

or Separation?

By Doug Belkin - P. B. Post 2000

While the black professional class quadrupled between 1954 and 1990, the percentage of black children born into poverty has increased from 43% in 1968 to 47% in the year 2000 according to the US census. Meanwhile one in four black men is in trouble with the law and one in five is in college. Black men are more likely to be jailed, to receive the death penalty and to be killed by homicide than their white counterparts. The black underclass has grown from 900,000 in 1982 2.7 million in 1995.

Bush knows the statistics like she knows her own name. She is a veteran of civil rights movement and lifelong community activist with enough plaques of appreciation in her house to wallpaper her living room. She remembers the days of King and Malcolm and Bobby and occasionally speaks of them in the present tense. She is a woman that does not walk two blocks in West Palm Beach without saying hello to someone and asking after their mother. Though she is retired from a long career as an elementary school teacher, she's busier now than she ever was.

But the world is not fixed, she says. There are culprits who have conspired to turn Seventh and Tamarind into an ill kept, open-air drug market. There are the politicians who distribute money in city services unevenly, the police who intimidate, harass and protect selectively, the clergy who have failed to lead, a community that silently condones it all by lowering expectations, the men in themselves who make bad choices, and the media who adulate the destructive role models which black teenagers aspire.

Will the race gap in America close in her lifetime? Bush says. "Not until aggressive people take aggressive roles."

Thirty-two years after King was killed, Bush says there aren't enough of those leaders, especially in the clergy. Last summer Bush tried to organize area churches to help clean up her old neighborhood. Forty-two invitations went out to 42 churches; four pastors showed up.

"The old generation of leadership is dying out in the next generation There is a great silence out there and I don't know why. I wish I did."

There is a speech known as the Joshua Sermon delivered in black churches around this time every year to coincide with Martin Luther King Day. The subject is that silence: Moses was chosen by God to lead the Jews out of slavery in Egypt, the minister will say, just as King was chosen by God to lead African-Americans out of the psychological slavery that 400 years and change perpetuated.

Moses climbed the mountain top to look across the promised land, the minister will say; so did King. Moses died before he entered that promise land, the minister will say again; so did King.

Without Moses did you wander in the wilderness, waiting for a new leader to come along and take them home? The new leader was Joshua, who, as every Sunday school student is told, boke down the walls of Jericho and led his people into the promised land of milk and honey.

Many liters, not only one.

The black community, the minister will say, is still in that wilderness, still suffering from that leadership vacuum, still waiting for that next anointed leader to lead them to their promised land.

"What King did was he was able to unify the black community nationwide, and that's a focus we don't have right now," and said Rev. Spivey of the Lake Ida Church of Christ in Delray Florida. "Jesse Jackson made an effort, but he does not have the same stature as King, and I don't think you can train someone to do it. I think a leader like that comes along ever so often, almost at God's will. King wasn't even the movement's 1st choice, but was the man that God selected, just like Moses and now we need to anoint a man to take us across the Jordan. That's what we are waiting for."

"It's an interesting theory, this idea of a prophetic leader," says the Reverend Gerald Kisner of the Tabernacle Missionary Baptist Church, "but it's not one that he accepts. Up the hill from the intersection at Seventh and Tamarind is the Tabernacle—a massive white church that exudes the decorum that Mrs. Bush is talking about. Surrounding the church are 53 homes in various stages of construction that may breathe new life into the neighborhood," Rev. Kisner said.

These sort of projects, Kisner says, are where the rubber meets the road. It doesn't take a messiah to get them going. "If King came back today, I think he'd have problems," Kisner said. "King was a visionary but someone else had to implement that vision and that's what we are trying to do. That's what needs to be done. We need to stop complaining and start acting."

"That implementation," Kisner argues, "needs to come from a broad base of support, not a single person. One leader—however charismatic—can be assassinated or brought off or corrupted. A generation of leaders is not so easily turned back."

Still a generation of leaders needs to be groomed, and then the cross currents of competing agendas and philosophies and distraction that is not so easily accomplished.

A legacy betrayed. "If King was alive today, he would be disappointed," Edith C. Bush says. "There are still people out there like Jackson and Sharpton who have the fiber of a Reverend King, but they've been worn down and there's not too many people helping them out."

CHAPTER 21

West Palm Beach Activist Leads

Effort To Honor Dr. King

By Belinda Brockman – P. B. Post, 1991

In West Palm Beach, Edith C. Bush, too, has a dream. "All we need to do is understand each other, and we can make the world a better place to live."

For all her life Mrs. Bush worked to keep that dream thriving. She helped lead the Black Educator Caucus of the Palm Beach County Classroom Teachers Association efforts to honor Martin Luther King, Jr., starting in 1971. For the last four years, she has been chairwoman of the West Palm Beach Martin Luther King, Jr. Coordinating Committee.

To us he made the Bible a living example," Bush said. "Author and philosophers have written many things, but they have not shown it in reality. Dr. King actually gave an example of what Christ really meant. This year's 1991 celebration, leading up to the Monday's national holiday recognizing the civil rights leader, begin with the reception January 10. It's art exhibit, an interfaith service, a tennis tournament, and an oratorical contest. A gospel fest will be held today and the annual essay awards breakfast is Monday.

" Our objective is to continually remind the public, the nation, of the principles of Dr. King," Bush said.

"We are very proud of the result of our activities. Charles Ellington has been involved with local King day activities often through the years and is working with Bush on January 10 reception.

Bush watched her country lurch from Jim Crow to the modern era. There has been progress, she says, even if it is now becoming clear to all that Black people face systemic racism.

Bush placed the blame for the persistence of systemic racism on the judicial system because so many issues, such as punishment for crime, fairness and housing or education go through it.

She believes the country should do away with lifetime appointments for the Supreme Court and other judicial appointments, because you can't have someone "whose mind is still in the 40s."

As she sees it, if the President of the United States can be term limited, then justices should be too.

Insider networking also has kept qualified Black people out of jobs, she believes.

Amidst all this, she believes the current wave approaches will push progress along. The death of George Floyd, Breonna Taylor and Sandra Bland, among others, have brought attention to many of the inequalities in the justice system, Bush says.

"I know it's going to be meaningful change," she says. "You have new people now who are going to be looking at everything—including contracts, qualifications."

It is very important to get qualified African-Americans and keep positions, she says.

Turning to voting in the recent debacle in Georgia, Bush says the malfunctions that tend to occur in minority and poor communities highlight "the fact that there is unfairness in this country."

She also remains concerned about the upkeep of many minority communities. "We are paying taxes to improve our community and it's not being done. If they were upscale communities, it would be done."

Noting the importance of voting, Bush is convinced that protests inspired by Floyd's death will last. "I think these protests will continue through November because every effort is going to be made to prevent people from voting."

As shabby as they were, the colored restrooms were preferable to no restroom at all. "It really hurts sometimes when we had to stop on the side of the road or behind bushes because you wouldn't be allowed in some restrooms," Bush says.

While at Bethune Cookman College, where she attended on a combination of tuition and a work scholarship, Bush's tasks included getting Mary McLeod Bethune's home ready whenever she visited the campus.

She finally recalls that "I had the privilege of meeting Eleanor Roosevelt and Marian Anderson. Dr. Bethune brought them to the campus."

She earned her degree in elementary education – because, well, that was the most common career path for Black people, particularly women, back then. She later completed a Master's Degree in Education at Florida Atlantic University.

A widow, she has a daughter, Lavette Robinson who lives with her, and two grandchildren, Miranda and Julian, who live in Tennessee.

Bush spent 32 years in Palm Beach County schools before retiring in 1987, but she hasn't slowed down.

" It's going to be meaningful change."

She is a member of the Anytime Church of God in Christ, a member of the Equal Justice Initiative established by Attorney Brian Stevenson, and Martin Luther King, Jr. Coordinating Committee. The committee helps plan the annual MLK Breakfast, which brings prominent speakers to West Palm Beach.

Whether it's organizing a bus trip to Washington for President Barack Obama's inauguration or heading to Sanford to protest the killing of Treyvon Martin, Bush is always finding a cause to get behind.

The recent marches are no exceptions. She has a Black Lives Matter T-shirt, and despite the fact that her age puts her in high-risk group for coronavirus, she attended a small demonstration in support of racial justice on the steps of the courthouse in West Palm Beach in early June.

The event was organized by the Palm Beach County Clergy Alliance, which appealed to Bush's deep religious background.

She also witnessed a large protest at Currie Park. She stayed in her car and watched the protesters march by. She has pictures of that day.

CHAPTER 22

Achievers Award Winners

See Hard Work on Equality Ahead
By Andrew Abrahamson – P. B. Post – May 3, 2012

More than a decade after the Martin Luther King, Jr. Landmark Memorial Park debuted on Flagler Drive in Currie Park, Edith C. Bush and Samuel Bruce McDonald still marvel at its symbolism.

Bush and McDonald, who beat out hundreds of South Florida applicants last month to become two of the four JM Family Enterprises African American Achievers, still remember a different time in West Palm Beach when they fought just to gain acceptance. A memorial on Flagler wasn't even a thought.

We've come a long way, says Bush, 79, who won this year's culture award. As proud as Bush is about advancement of the black community in recent decades, winning this prestigious award came at a crucial time, she said. "We still have a long way to go, hatred is rising in this country because of a black president being in the White House." Bush has made King's memory a huge part of her life.

In 1971, the establishment of the Martin Luther King Jr. Coordinating Committee was made, an organization in West Palm Beach that promotes King's legacy through cultural activities, art exhibits and youth programs.

While King is never far from her mind, these days Bush is focusing on President Obama's reelection efforts.

"This is an awesome year. This is a huge year. It is a huge year with so many efforts out there to defeat Obama and the effort to minimize African American votes by states initiating ID laws."

Bush attended several Trayvon Martin rallies across the state, and said she believes "the Martin shooting has galvanized black voters" and is going to become an important issue in the election.

The African American Achievers Awards Program was established in 1992 to recognize everyday heroes who make a difference in the lives of others.

The honorees chosen from more than 350 nominations, were selected by an independent panel of community leaders from Miami-Dade, Broward and Palm Beach counties.

JM Family, Southeast Toyota and JM Lexus donated $40,000 to non-profit organizations—$10,000 to the organization of each honoree's choice.

CHAPTER 23

Edith C. Bush

American Legion Auxiliary Blog

The ALA Stories blog series showcases positive American Legion Auxiliary experiences, thoughts, and ideas of ALA members. We hope these blogs will inspire and encourage all who read them.

At 89 years old, Edith C. Bush has lived through decades when the daily chances of her, or other black Americans, encountering some form of discrimination was a certain as the sun rising each day.

America's long gone legalized racial segregation, which bolstered the evil doctrine of white supremacy, was in place for much of Bush's life. The resulting overt and covert oppression of black Americans was the norm in those days. Add to that race-based inequities, harassment, death threats, and unwarranted violence—sometimes lethal, all aimed at black Americans.

Bush could have cloaked her heart in a shroud of hatred aimed at all white people. But she never did. Bush could have stopped loving America when it seemed like America did not love her back. But she never did. Instead, Bush chose a path of harmony and unity among all people, in all parts of life. She's naturally driven to help anyone in need. Bush continues to love America, plus its principles of freedom, democracy, and equality.

She is optimistic that our nation will remain on its path toward a more just union for all of its people. And, she cares deeply for those who protect and defend the United States and its interests.

Bush does all of this as a member of the American Legion auxiliary, a community of volunteers serving veterans, military, and their families. "We want to make sure our veterans are taken care of, whether it's picking up their medication when they can't, making sure they have food, or whatever. We have to do these things for them if they need help because they did something for all of us: they served our country. We need to be inclusive in our membership in order to serve all," said Bush, a longtime member of ALA unit 199 in West Palm Beach FL. "I'm excited to be a part of ALA because we are associated with organizations that can provide help for military people and their families. I love to help people! That's my thing! If those in need are having their needs for filled, that makes me happy," she added. I'm a three-F person: faith, family, and friends.

"We need to be inclusive in our membership in order to serve all."

-ALA member Edith C. Bush

PART 4

*

Where Are They Now?

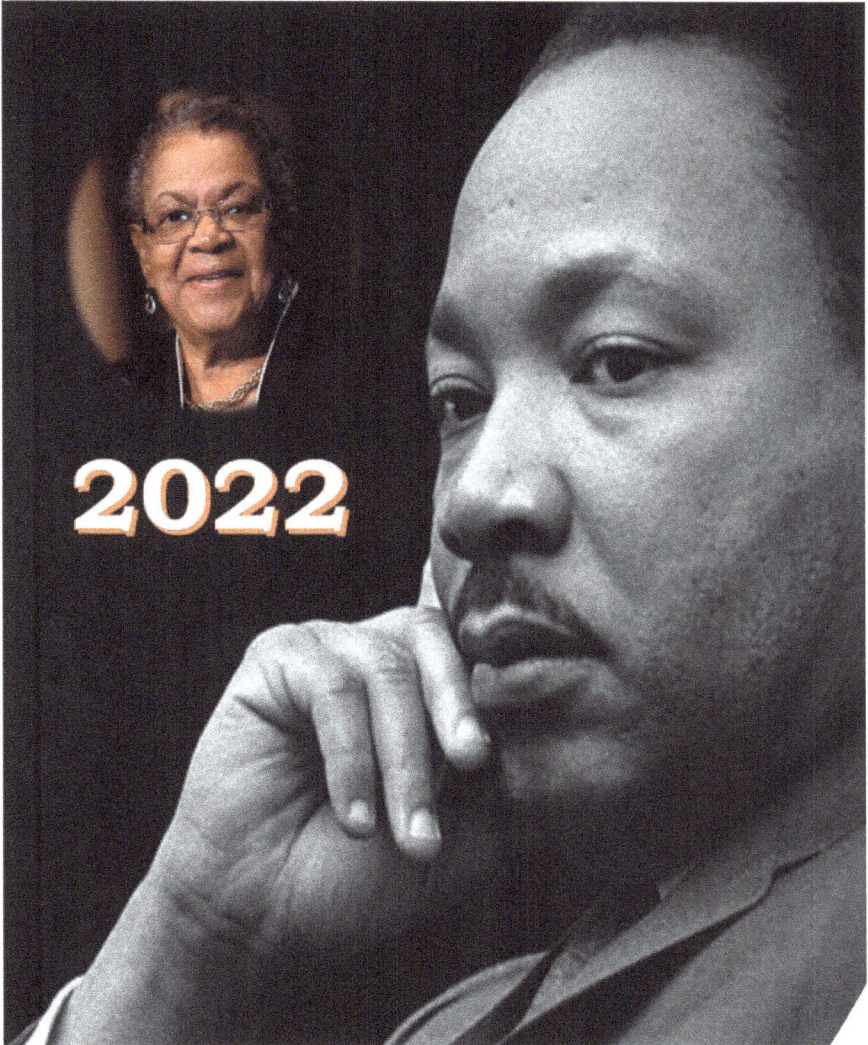

The Martin Luther King, Jr Coordinating Committee
Student Award Winners

WHERE ARE THEY NOW?

- MLK Scholarship Recipient
- 2022 Inaugural "Where Are They Now" Video Montage Producer
- Performing Arts Committee Member
- Professional Chef

Shonse' K. Joseph

- Founder of MLK Performing Arts Contest
- MLK Coordinating Committee Member
- Coordinator of 2022 Inaugural
"Where Are They Now" Montage
- Speaker, Performer at MLK events

Rev. Iona Joseph-Gamble

Pastor
Jeremiah Chester

Oratorical Contest
Senior Pastor of
St. Mark Baptist Church
in Huntsville, AL

Elvin J. Dowling

Oratorical Contest
Award-Winning Author
and Activist

Terrell Evans

Oratorical Contest
Palm Beach County
Fire Rescue Employee

Prophet Bryce Graham

Performing Arts Contest
Community Activist

Sandria Harris

Performing Arts Contest
Florida Atlantic University
Senior

Tyrielle Jarmon

Oratorical Contest
Mentor for EmpowHER
Leadership Academy for Girls

Shayla Knighton-Black

Performing Arts Contest
Florida A&M University
Doctoral student

Diva Koon

Oratorical Contest
Palm Beach County
Convention Center Employee

Brealauna "Breezy" Leassear

Oratorical, Essay, Art,
Performing Arts Contests
Receiving Coordinator
Costco

Noble Lockhart-Mays

Performing Arts Contest
A vocalist
Director of Faith's Place Center
for Education

Anthawney McDowell

Oratorical Contest
Martin Luther King Coordinating
Committee
Summer Peace Camp Director
School District of Palm Beach County
Employee

Annique Joielle Owens

Performing Arts Contest
Speech and Language Pathologist
School District of Palm Beach
County

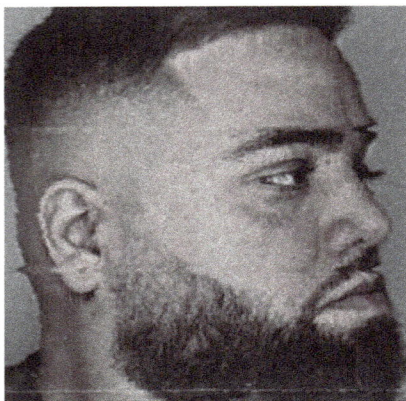

Juan Pino

Performing Arts Contest
Gospel Recording Artist

Linnie Supall

Oratorical Contest
Reporter for WPTV
Channel 5 News

Tamera Tysinger

Performing Arts Contest
University of Central Florida
Sophomore

Julio Vega

Performing Arts Contest
Los Angeles Recording School
Student

Bishop Ricardo Weaver, Sr.

Performing Arts
and Oratorical Contests
Senior Pastor of City Church
Mortuary Science Student at
Gupton-Jones College

Cameren Anai Williams

Performing Arts Contest
Student at Julliard School of Music
Author and Private Teacher
Violin And Viola

Ervin Williams

Oratorical, Performing Arts,
Poetry, and Essay Contests
Wheaton College
Sophomore

Melissa Wright

Oratorical Contest
Business Manager
Property Management Groups

RoShanta M. Wright-Cone

Oratorical Contest
Owner, Dot Rose Couture
Specializes in custom,
made-to-order garments

Sherrita Edwards Tommie

Performing Arts Contest
Entrepreneur and Operator
SLT Real Estate & Investments, LLC.

Dr. Kali D. Cyrus

Dr. Kali Cyrus is one of the few Black, queer, female, Ivy League educated psychiatrists on the market, and she offers groundbreaking consultation on managing conflicts stemming from identity differences. She grew up in West Palm Beach and graduated from Suncoast Community High School in 2002. She received her BA in Psychology from Stanford University, Masters in Public Health from Emory University, and Medical Degree from the University of Illinois at Chicago. She completed psychiatric training at the Yale School of Medicine and served on the faculty. She is a respected leader in highlighting the ways in which discrimination impacts health through her political advocacy with the Committee to Protect Medicare, academically as an Assistant Professor at Johns Hopkins Medicine, and in the mainstream media using videos and speaking engagements, including national news outlets like CNN and MSNBC.

Kali D. Cyrus M.D., M.P.H. Consultant, Psychiatrist

Part 5
Pictorial History

Martin Luther King, Jr. Landmark Memorial Park

Martin Luther King, Jr. Coordinating Committee

Dr. Martin Luther King, Jr. Landmark Memorial Park 2400 N. Flagler Dr., West Palm Beach

CONTRIBUTORS

Nancy M Graham

Howard Worshire

Mary B. Hooks

Joel T. Daves

Alfred Zucaro, Jr.

John F. Jeff Koons

Jorge Avellana

Cinthia Becton

Bevins Bennett, Jr

Mary Lawrence Brabham

Geneva Brooks

Phyllis Brooks

Rev. John B Brown

Dorothy Darling

Bettye Dawson

Dr. Othelia Dubose

Charlie Ellington

Iona Gamble

Amefika Geuka

Olga Wallace-Gideon

Susan Owen Glaser

Nancy Graham

Lucius Hamilton

Jill Hanson

Annie Ruth Harrison

Judy Hasner

Jim Horne

Susan Jewel

Rev. Frank Jefferson

Elizabeth M Johnson

Jeff Koons

Ronald Leonard

Carolyn Lester

E Yvonne K Littles

Rev. W. Ivey Mack

Luciano Martinez

Rev. I. F. Mitchell

Dr. Alice E. Moore

Emma L. Moore

Charlotte Pelton

Frank Polk

Erma T. Porter

Debbye Raing

Ken Rearden

Gladys Reed

Raul Rio

Billy L. Rozier

Sara Schlissberg

Flip Schulke

Laura Schuppert

Gloria Shuttlesworth

Sol Silverman

Jacqueline Smith

Mary Sweigart

Elaine Troy

Ernest Washington

Roy Washington

Desmond Williamson

Shirley Wright

Mary Jane Zapp

Edith C. Bush (seated) Family Reunion
Okeechobee City, FL

2012 African-American Achievers with
President & CEO, Colin Brown
J.M. Enterprises

Daughter Lavette Robinson, Nephew Senator
Bobby Powell, Jr. and Edith C. Bush

2012 Arts & Culture Achiever
Calvin Hughes, Presenter
J.M. Enterprises

Edith Bush with
President & CEO, Colin Brown
and Jan Moran
J.M. Enterprises

AraJean Ross, Katherine Marshall, Alvin Edward Coleman, Pauline C. Spears, Edith C. Bush. Willie Lee Crumpley

Andalusian enjoys Caribbean cruise

Will Coleman enjoyed a cruise to the Carribean-Bahama Islands, via the SS Amerikanis cruise ship recently.

He was accompanied by his daughter and son-in-law, Mr. and Mrs. Alvin (Edith) Bush Jr. of West Palm Beach, Fla.

While in Nassau, Bahamas, the group visited the famous straw markets, toured the island and were

entertained at the famous Paradise Island Casino Resort. The resort is known for its Las Vegas simulated shows.

"The trip was an educational experience. Also, the gourmet dining was superb," Mr. Coleman said.

He returned to Andalusia in time to enjoy Thanksgiving with his family.

Alvin Bush, Jr. husband; Edith C. Bush, Andalusian Will Coleman, father aboard the SS Amerikanis cruise ship

Berry - Coleman Family Reunion Pauline Spears and daughter; Katherine Marshall and daughter; Edith C. Bush and daughter

108

View of Will Coleman Recreation Center in Andalusia AL

Closeup view of the Will Coleman Recreation Center in Andalusia AL

Sabrina Cornish and Collegues, Florida Neighborhoods Conference, St. Petersburg FL Edith C. Bush,

Sabrina Cornish and Edith C. Bush, at the Dr. Cartter G. Woodson African American History Musuem in St. Petersburg FL

Edith C. Bush at the Women's International League for Peace and Freedom

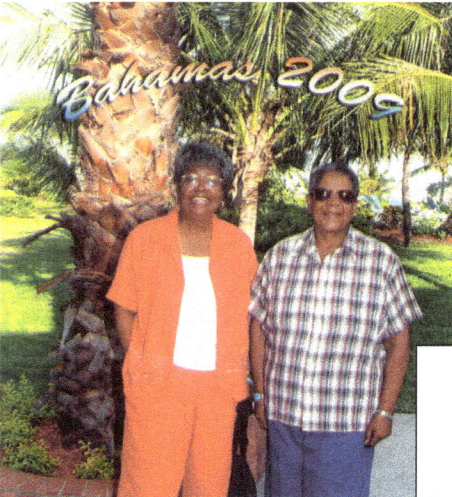

Betty T. Dawson and Edith C. Bush on vacation in Nassau Bahamas

Edith C. Bush visits the White House in Washington D.C.

Edith C. Bush visiting the Holocaust Memorial in Miami, FL

Edith C. Bush (center) poses with the Progressive Northwest Neighborhood Association

Edith C. Bush, Founder and Executive Director of the Martin L. King Jr. Coordinating Committee speaks before groundbreaking Ceremony

Rev. Fred Shuttlesworth (not shown) of Birmingham, AL Pastor of 16th Street Baptist Church was at the unveiling in January 1997

MLKCC marches crowd from the MLK Landmark Memorial dedication

Guitar performance with Mayor Lois Frankel and Edith C. Bush at MLK Landmark Memorial {24AB}

Mary B. Hooks unveils the Dr. Martin Luther King, Jr. Memorial {32}

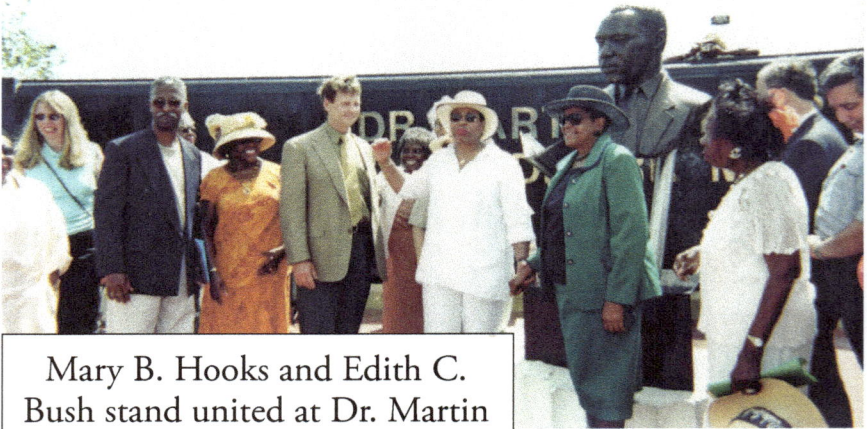

Mary B. Hooks and Edith C. Bush stand united at Dr. Martin Luther King, Jr. Memorial

People

Executive Director at the Lake Worth Guatemalan-Maya Center uses family centered approach

CIVIL DUTY: Susan Glaser is the Executive Director at the Guatemalan-Maya Center in Lake Worth. She started as a volunteer in 1992 when the center opened its doors to the Guatemalan-Mayan community.

Staff photo/ Jackie Gerena

Executive Director, Lake Worth Guatemalan-Maya Center, Susan Glaser

By MICHAEL DAVIS
FORUM STAFF WRITER

The Guatemalan-Maya Center, Inc in Lake Worth serves a local population of people that have fled their native Guatemala due to an era of political violence and genocide launched against the Maya in the late 1980's and early 1990's.

Lake Worth resident Susan Glaser is the executive director of the Guatemalan-Maya Center, located at 110 North F St.

The goal of the center according to Glaser is to create an environment where families and children can explore their potential possibilities in an American lifestyle without abandoning the Maya culture.

"The center serves as a bridge between the Maya people and the American society," Glaser said. "The public is often surprised that many Maya here speak no Spanish or no English, only their indigenous Maya languages."

The Guatemalan-Maya Center was founded in 1992 to provide a center for Maya refugees. It

was determined at that time that many of the state and local agencies thought the Maya were Hispanics. Even the Immigration and Naturalization Services did not know what to do with the Maya refugees and the INS accepted political asylum cases but kept these cases in a pending motion. Many refugees are still waiting for resolution of their cases. This places the Maya in consistent limbo, which makes it difficult for the Maya to fully participate in the American society.

Glaser said the stories that she has heard are horrific and traumatic.

"Every person that I have talked to has witnessed the murder of his or her grandfather, father, brother or husband," she said. "Besides witnessing horrific crimes, there is the additional traumatic experience from their trip across the border into Mexico and then the cultural shock here in the states."

Glaser is responsible for the day-to-day operation of the organization per instruction from the board of directors. Many of the current board members were involved in the formation of the

center.

A major component of the center is the pre- and post-natal program. The center also runs two after school care programs in Lake Worth and Boynton Beach with more than 120 children of Maya descent participating.

Although there is no way to know exactly how many Maya live in Lake Worth, Glaser said the center got a good indication after Hurricane Frances hit Palm Beach County.

"There were estimates of about 5,000 Maya here in Lake Worth," she said. "The county population is somewhere around 40,000."

The staff of nearly 40 works with the Maya on obtaining documents such as photo IDs.

"The Maya are a very special group of people," Glaser said. "They are very family oriented and many times when they do come to the center for help it's an emergency. It really shows how resilient the Maya are."

For more information, call 561-547-0085.

Michael Davis can be reached at mwdavis@tribune.com.

114

Lois Frankel with honorees at MLKCC Scholarship Breakfast 2005

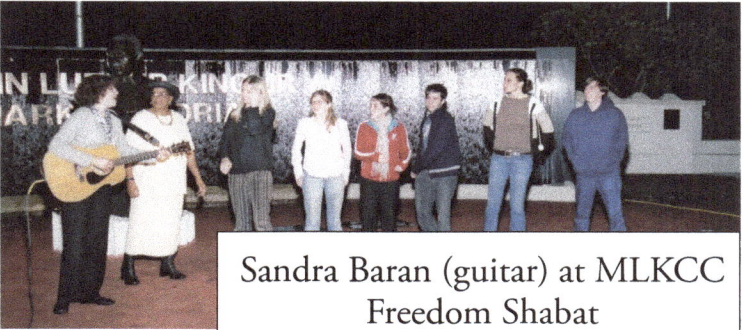

Sandra Baran (guitar) at MLKCC Freedom Shabat

Freedom Shabat 2005 at MLK Landmark Memorial sponsord by Pax Christi - St. Ann Catholic Church

Art Awardees at Roosevelt
Elementary School - Dr. Glenda
Garrett Principal

Edith C. Bush & Hyacinthia
Becton with Performing Arts
Awardees 2005

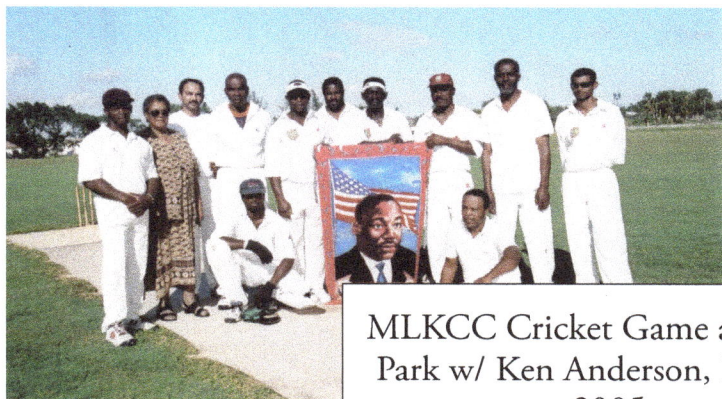

MLKCC Cricket Game at Gaines Park w/ Ken Anderson, Director 2005

Unity Service at Emmanuel MB Church in Mangnia Park, FL - Rev Erick Evans, Pastor

Candlelight Service at MLK Landmark Memorial 2005

Kickoff Reception at Grace Episcopal Church - WPB Vandry Chin, Edith C. Bush, Sallie Belk

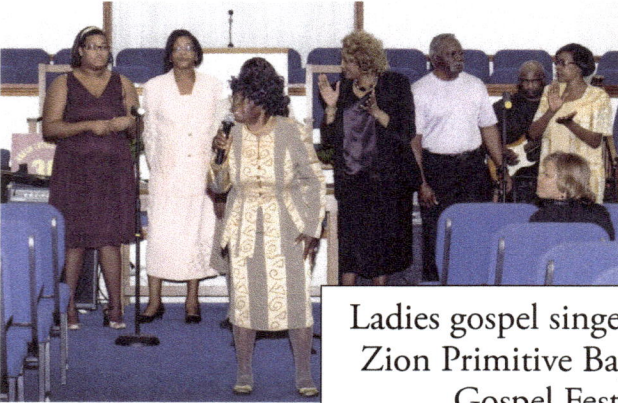

Ladies gospel singers at Orthodox Zion Primitive Baptist Church - Gospel Fest Service

MLKCC honors Dixie Printing Company, Priscilla Taylor & Hyacinthia Becton

Freedom Celebration
Praise Dancers at
St. Ann Catholic Church

Mens gospel singers at Orthodox
Zion Primitive Baptist Church -
Gospel Fest Service

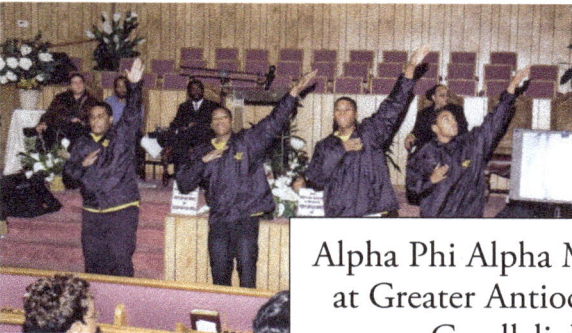

Alpha Phi Alpha Men of Tomorrow
at Greater Antioch MB Church -
Candlelight Service

Art Awards Committee at Palm Beach County Classroom Teachers Association - Annie R. Nelson Committee Chair

District Representative Bobby Powell, Jr

Freedom Shabat at Temple Israel WPB

Violin selection from
Performing Arts
contestant

Gregg Weiss, Sylvia Moffett, Bobby Powell, Jr.,
Nina Holland with Performing Arts winners 2015

Faith's Place performing
at the Performing Arts
competition

Oratorical Winner
Sterling Shipp 2015

Gregg Weiss, Annie Ruth Nelson,
Betty T. Dawson, and Ray White
at Art awards reception 2015

Brealauna
"Breezy"
Leasscar, Edith
C. Bush, Betty
T. Dawson, and
Patricia Johnson
- Oratorical
Contest

MLKCC at Temple Israel WPB - Freedom Shabatt Celebration

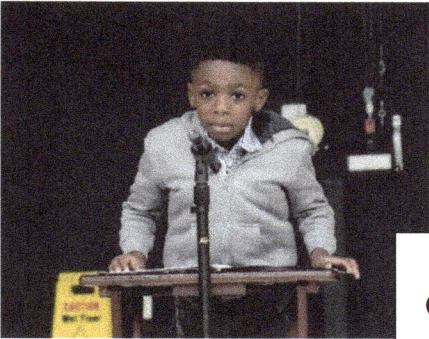

Darren Blake
Oratorical performer

Victoria Lawrence oratorical winner with Sylvia Moffett, Betty T. Dawson, and Edith C. Bush

Cecil Cooper with a student at Health & Safety Fair

Health & Safety Fair - Blood Drive group performance at MLK Landmark Memorial

Edith C. Bush,
Founder/ Executive Director
of Martin Luther King, Jr.
Coordinating Committee

Dominick Simmons,
Student athlete, Motorcity Thunder
Basketball, Detroit
Multiple Award Winner

www.ingramcontent.com/pod-product-compliance
Lightning Source LLC
Chambersburg PA
CBHW051213090426
42742CB00021B/3434

* 9 7 8 1 7 3 5 3 8 2 8 4 5 *